Pilot Ollie & Pilot Polly's Amazing Adventures

www. planecharacters.com

Ticket Hunt!

See if you can find all the Boarding Passes!

There are many ways of getting to the airport.

You can catch a train or a bus or maybe drive and park your car in one of the big car parks.

Sometimes you will need to catch a bus or little train from the car park to the main airport terminal building.

Some airports have lots of terminals so you have to make sure you go to the right one.

TH TERMINAL
3
2
PARKING

When you walk into the terminal you will need to look for the signs saying “Departures”.

If your bags and suitcases are very heavy you can put them on a trolley or get a porter to help you. Sometimes it can be a very long walk as airports are huge places.

DEPARTURES
ARRIVAL
STUFF
Eat & Run

When you find the departures area you will see a line of desks called check-in desks. Chelsey Checker is a check-in assistant and sits at one of these desks. She will be able to help you check in for your flight.

“Can I see your ticket and passport please?” She’ll say. You need a passport to travel to different countries.

It has your photo and birthday in it so the other countries can recognise you.

Chelsey Checker will press some buttons on her computer and print out your boarding passes.

Chelsey Checker puts your bags on the conveyor belt by her desk and weighs them. Larry Loader needs to know how heavy your bags are so he can balance the plane when he loads them in to the cargo holds.

Chelsey Checker will put a tag on your bag which has a special barcode on it. The tag will also have your name and destination on it.

Every airport in the world has a three letter code. If you are going to Amsterdam the code would be AMS.

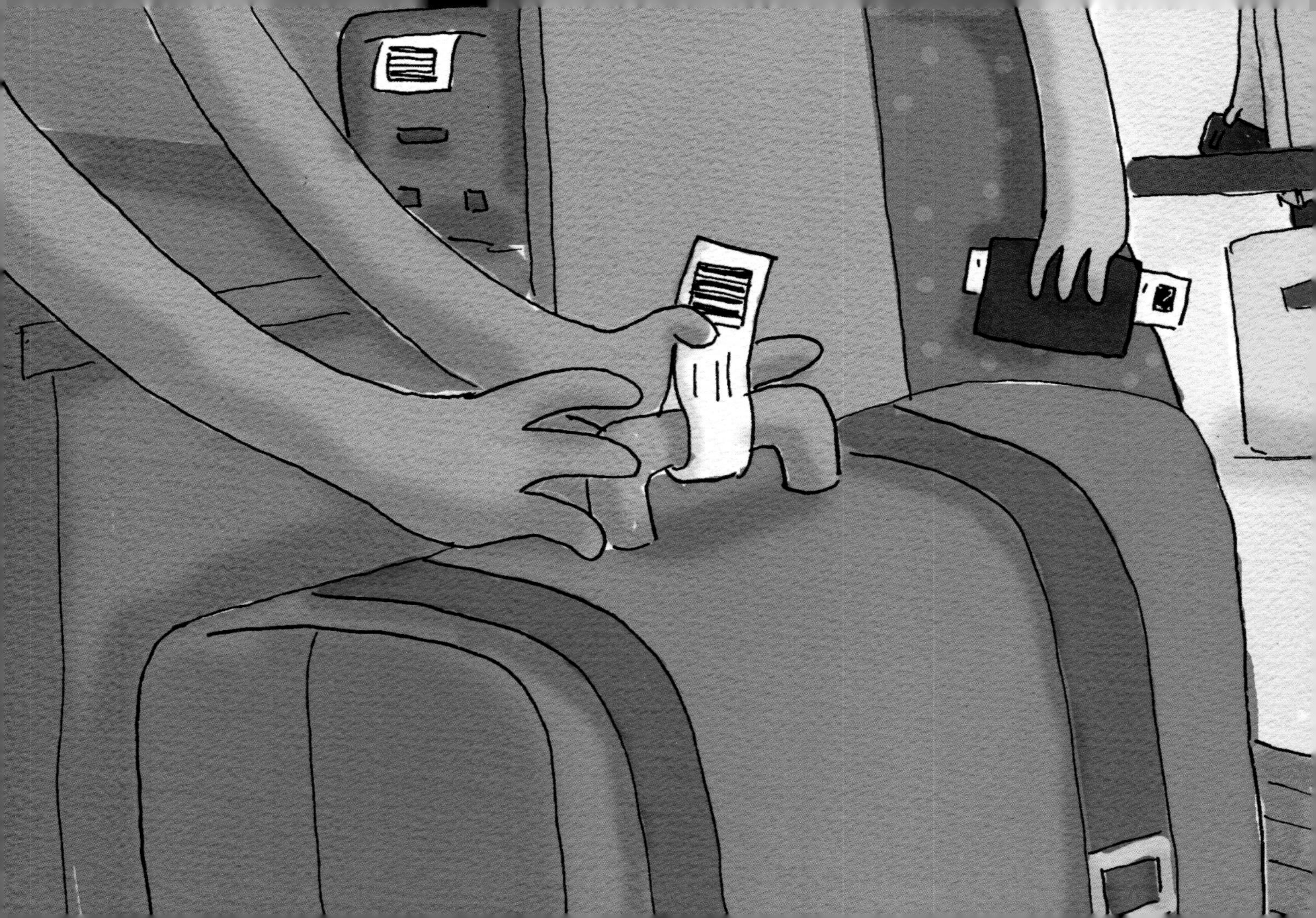

When your suitcases are weighed and tagged Chelsey Checker will press a button on her check-in desk and your bags will whizz off on the conveyor belt. You won't see your bags again until you arrive at your destination.

Your bags will whizz along on fast conveyor belts. The special barcode on the tag is scanned by computerised tag readers.

They send signals to the computerised gates on the conveyor belts that open and close and send your bag to the right place for your flight.

Larry Loader will be waiting for your bag to arrive on the conveyor belt. When it arrives he will put it on his baggage truck and wait for the other passenger's bags.

On some of the bigger aircrafts the bags are put into big metal boxes called "Bins." The bins are then taken out to the aircraft and loaded onto the cargo hold.

When all the bags have arrived, Larry Loader will jump into his truck and tow the trailers full of bags out to the aircraft.

He always drives very slowly so that the bags do not fall off. If it is raining he can cover the bags with a roof.

In the airport terminal the next sign you will need to look for is "Security". There might be a queue of people here.

You will probably have to take off your shoes and empty your pockets out before you walk through the x-ray scanner.

Sometimes the scanners go "Beep!" as you walk through and the security officer will ask to check your arms and legs. When they do this it tickles!

The small bag that you are taking onto the plane with you will also have to go through an x-ray machine.

A conveyor belt similar to the one your suitcase went on takes your bag through the machine. Sometimes you might be able to see an x-ray picture of your bag. Don’t forget to collect your bag after the x-ray and put your shoes on!

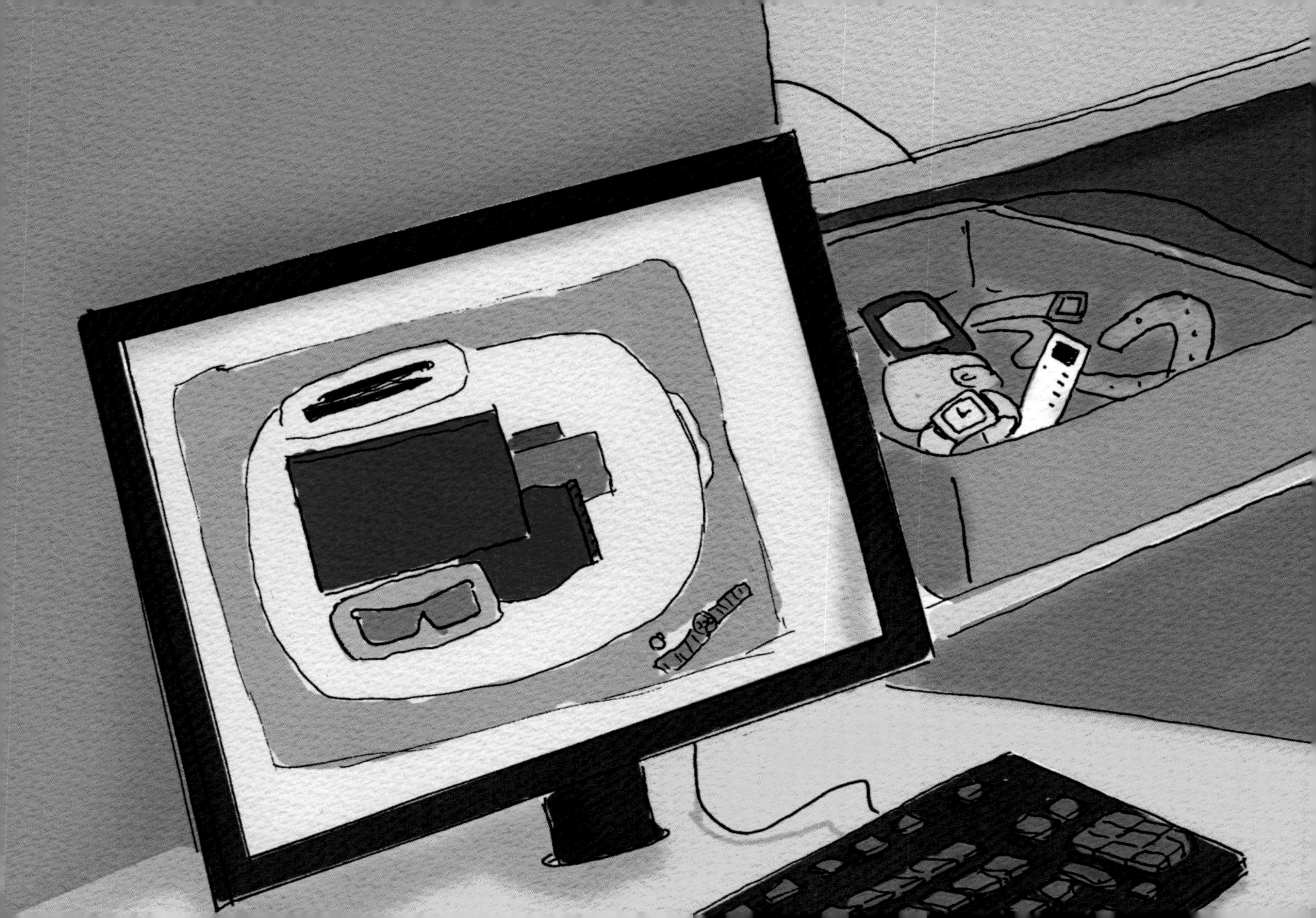

You will now be in the departure lounge. There are usually shops and cafes in the departure lounge where you can have a rest and sometimes there is a play area.

Some departure lounges have big windows and if you look out you might be able to see your plane. You might also be able to see lots of special airport vehicles driving around.

Your pilots, Pilot Ollie and Pilot Polly, will have arrived at the airport too. They have a special area in the airport terminal where they check their bags in and go through security just like you will have done.

Woody Weatherman will have drawn up some weather charts for Pilot Ollie and Pilot Polly, and Chris Controller will have produced a map for them to follow.

Sometimes at really big airports there is more than one departure lounge. Your boarding card will tell you where to go and you will need to follow the signs.

It might be a long walk or there may be a moving walkway, a bus, monorail or a small train to take you there. If you look out of the windows you might be able to see the airport workers doing their jobs.

GATE 52

Alfie Engineer will have checked your plane. He always has a good look at the plane's wheels and brakes and tops up the oil in the plane's engines.

Today he is standing on some steps and cleaning the plane's windscreens so Pilot Ollie and Pilot Polly can see where they are going.

Under the plane's wing Freddy Fueller has connected his tanker to the plane with a big hose. The tanker pumps fuel into the plane's wings where it is stored.

Some airports have underground fuel pipes and so a smaller pumping truck is used to connect between the fuel pipes and the plane.

Onboard your plane, a team of cleaners are vacuuming the floors and polishing the walls to make it look sparkling and new.

The caterers will be taking off all the old food and drink and loading fresh new snacks for you. As the cleaners finish up the security team search the plane and then the cabin crew can get onboard.

Mike, Megan and Molly will be your cabin crew today. The cabin crew are also known as flight attendants.

They are on board the plane to serve you snacks and drinks. They are also qualified first aiders and there is a first aid kit with plasters in just in case you hurt yourself.

The cabin crew will complete their safety checks and then Pilot Ollie and Pilot Polly arrive.

Pilot Ollie will put his flight case in the plane's flightdeck and then walks around the outside of the plane. He will have a good look at the wheels, tyres and the brakes.

He will also have a look at the huge engines to make sure they are ready for the flight.

Pilot Polly will be having a good look at the maps that Chris Controller has given her and programs the plane’s computers.

The computers need to know where they are starting and where they are going. Pilot Polly will also start the small jet engine in the plane’s tail that provides power and cool air to the cabin.

In the departure lounge there are big TV screens showing all the flights that are leaving that day.

You need to look through the list of flights, find yours and see which door you need to go to. These doors are called departure gates.

DEPARTURES

International Flights

Time	Flight	Gate	Check in
10:30	ABC01	52	3
10:45	ABC05	34	
11:10	ABC10	10	2
11:30	ABC23	46	
12:00	ABC33	23	

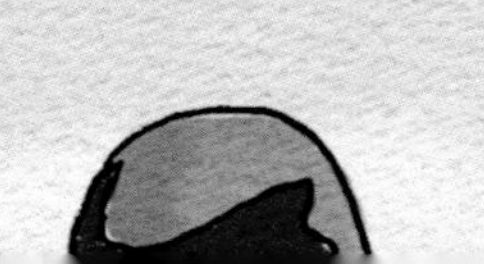

At the departure gate Chelsey Checker will be there to meet you. “Hello,” she’ll say, “I’m glad you found the departure gates.”

Chelsey Checker will ask to see your boarding pass to make sure you are at the right departure gate and scan it into the computer. Outside the window you might be able to see your plane being refuelled.

There is one person in overall charge of the plane's departure. Her name is Tara Turnaround. She is called the turnaround manager or sometimes the dispatcher.

She will be making sure that Freddie Fueller has put the fuel onboard, Larry Loader has put the suitcases in the cargo holds and that Pilot Ollie and Pilot Polly are ready.

When they are she will ring Chelsey Checker at the departure gate and tell her to let the passengers on. This is when you will be invited to walk down the bridge that connects the plane to the terminal and get onboard.

As you walk through the plane's big door you will be met by the cabin crew. Today Megan is standing by the door. "Welcome onboard," she says as she checks your boarding card, "you are sitting in the front row today in the seat by the window."

You will find lockers above your seat where you can store your small bag. If you look past the front door you might be able to see Pilot Ollie and Pilot Polly in the flightdeck programing the computers.

When all the passengers are onboard and Pilot Ollie and Pilot Polly are ready, Tara Turnaround will help Megan close the plane's big door.

Outside the plane Alfie Engineer will be checking that all the doors are closed and that the engines are ready.

He will remove the chocks from under the wheels and help the pushback tractor connect to the plane.

The plane is ready for departure. Pilot Ollie talks to Chris Controller on the plane’s radios. “This is Pilot Ollie requesting permission to start the big engines?” “You are cleared to start your engines,” says Chris Controller.

“**Chocks Away!**” Says Pilot Ollie as he starts the big jet engines. Once the engines have started Pilot Polly will request permission to taxi and takeoff and the plane with the crew and passengers onboard will fly off into the sky.

WHOOOOOSSHHHHHHH!!

Also Available